THE READ AGAIN & AGAIN OLD TESTAMENT BIBLE STORYBOOK

ILLUSTRATED BY
CHRIS JONES

FOCUS ON THE FAMILY.

A Focus on the Family
resource published by
Tyndale House Publishers

The READ AGAIN & AGAIN OLD TESTAMENT
BIBLE STORYBOOK

ILLUSTRATED BY
CHRiS JONes

"Let the little children come to me.
Don't keep them away.
God's kingdom belongs
to people like them."

Mark 10:14

TABLE OF CONTENTS

WELCOME, PARENTS!

Now more than ever, kids need to be equipped with the truth of the Bible from a young age. At *Focus on the Family Clubhouse Jr.* magazine, we've helped children engage with their faith and learn what it means to be a child of God for more than thirty-five years.

This book contains Old Testament Bible stories originally published in the pages of *Clubhouse Jr.* These visually engaging

stories were designed to grab your children's attention—the kinds of stories that kids will want to read again and again. As an added benefit, most of these stories feature a question or short takeaway for you to discuss together. Our goal is to help your children apply what they learn.

We pray that as your kids hear these stories, they'll grow in their love for God, their knowledge of the Bible, and their understanding of how God calls us to live—and love. We hope your entire family wants to read them again and again!

Blessings,
Jesse Florea
Editor, *Clubhouse Jr.*

IN THE BEGINNING

by Suzanne Gosselin • based on Genesis 1-2

In the beginning, God created the heavens and the earth. The earth was empty and dark. Water covered everything. There were no mountains, trees, animals or people.

God was there, though. His Spirit flew above the water. Then God spoke, "Let there be light."

Right away, light filled the earth. God separated the light from the dark and gave each a name. He called the light "day" and darkness "night."

That was the first day of God's creation.

God wasn't done. The next day, He said: "Let there be a huge space between the waters." And there was. God called the huge space "sky."

That was the second day of God's creation.

But God still had more to do! "Let dry ground appear," He said **on day three.** He called the dry ground "land" and the water around it "oceans." The land was plain. So God created plants and trees. Some had delicious fruit.

On day four, God added to the sky.

"Let there be lights in the huge space.... Let them serve as signs to mark off the seasons and the days and the years," He said.

God created the sun to shine brightly during the day. For the night, He created the moon to glow—and millions of sparkling stars.

The earth looked beautiful, but something was missing. **On the fifth day, God said: "Let the waters be filled with living things.** Let birds fly above the earth."

Suddenly, the oceans were overflowing with fish and whales. Birds soared across the sky.

God still wasn't done creating! On day six, God made animals to live in the fields and forests and mountains. Creatures crawled and scurried and galloped and hopped across God's beautiful earth.

These animals were amazing, but now God wanted to make His most special creation of all.

God formed together some dust of the ground. "Let us make man in our likeness," He said. God came near and gently breathed life into the man. God named him Adam. Then God created a woman who He named Eve. Both man and woman were made in God's image. Adam loved Eve very much. And God loved them both. That was the sixth day of God's creation.

On the seventh day, God had finished creating everything. So He rested. When God looked at His most special creation, He saw that it was very good.

God's Special Creation

God created everything in the universe. He made people who He could know and love. In return, the people could know, love and worship Him. That's why He created you! He knew you before you were born, and He loves you. You are His most special creation.

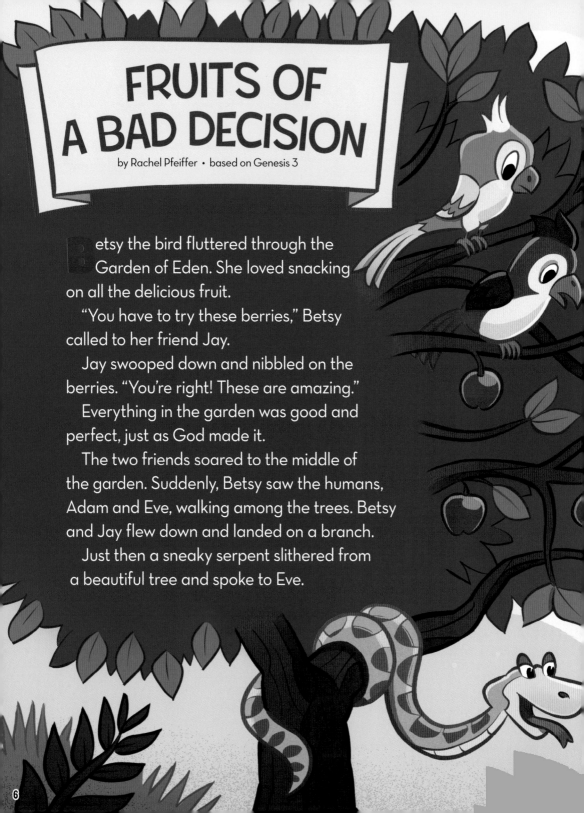

FRUITS OF A BAD DECISION

by Rachel Pfeiffer • based on Genesis 3

Betsy the bird fluttered through the Garden of Eden. She loved snacking on all the delicious fruit.

"You have to try these berries," Betsy called to her friend Jay.

Jay swooped down and nibbled on the berries. "You're right! These are amazing."

Everything in the garden was good and perfect, just as God made it.

The two friends soared to the middle of the garden. Suddenly, Betsy saw the humans, Adam and Eve, walking among the trees. Betsy and Jay flew down and landed on a branch.

Just then a sneaky serpent slithered from a beautiful tree and spoke to Eve.

"**D**id God really say, 'You must not eat fruit from any tree in the garden'?" the snake asked.

Eve shook her head. "We can eat the fruit from the trees," she said. "But God said if we eat fruit from this tree we will die."

"You will certainly not die," the snake said. "God knows when you eat fruit from this tree, you will know things you have never known before. You will be like God."

"Don't listen to that snake!" Betsy called.

All Eve heard was *chirp, chirp.*

Adam didn't say anything. Neither did Eve. She picked a piece of fruit and took a bite. Then she handed Adam a piece. He disobeyed God and ate it too.

Betsy shivered. She knew it wasn't right.

Betsy watched Adam and Eve sew together leaves to make clothes. Then they hid in the bushes.

"What's going on?" Jay asked.

"I don't know," Betsy said. "I think God is coming."

"Where are you, Adam?" God asked.

Adam and Eve came out of hiding. They confessed to eating the fruit and not following God's command.

"But she gave it to me." Adam pointed at Eve.

"The serpent tricked me," Eve said, also trying to pass the blame. "That's why I ate the fruit."

God didn't want excuses. He wanted obedience. Because of Adam and Eve's bad choice, sin and death entered the world. God forced them to leave His perfect garden.

Betsy and Jay watched the sad humans walk away.

"Nothing will be the same," Jay said. "I can't believe that mean snake tricked them!"

Betsy flew into the air.

"No, it won't be the same," she agreed. "But God promised He would send someone to make everything right again. And God always keeps His promises."

A Perfect Promise

Because Adam and Eve disobeyed God, they suffered the consequences of their sin. Sin separates us from God. But God loves us so much that He promised someone would come to save the world from sin. That someone is God's Son, Jesus! Romans 5:18 says, "One man's sin brought guilt to all people. In the same way, one right act made people right with God. That one right act gave life to all people." Jesus died on the cross and rose again so we can be rescued from our sin. When we believe in Jesus Christ as our Savior, we have eternal life with God.

Noah stopped sweeping. "Do you hear that?"

"Hear what?" Noah's wife asked.

"Exactly," Noah said. "The rain stopped!"

Noah's three sons and their wives cheered.

Noah and his family had weathered a lot of storms together. They were mocked and teased as they built the ark on dry ground. They had to wait for God to bring the animals onto the boat. Then they faced 40 days and 40 nights of rain.

Finally, it had stopped!

"When can we get off this boat, Dad?" Ham asked.

"When God tells us," Noah replied.

"I don't think I can wait another day," Shem's wife said.

"We'll get through this together," Noah's wife said.

THE LONG WAIT

by The Lynn Sisters • based on Genesis 6:9-8:19

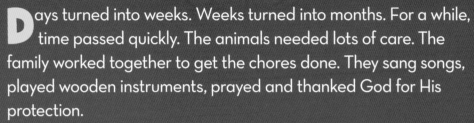

Days turned into weeks. Weeks turned into months. For a while, time passed quickly. The animals needed lots of care. The family worked together to get the chores done. They sang songs, played wooden instruments, prayed and thanked God for His protection.

Some days were harder. Noah's family didn't always get along. Sometimes they complained.

"Do you have to chew so loudly?" Japheth whined to Shem.

"Can't you sing a different song?" Shem asked Ham.

One day as the family ate dinner, they felt the boat jolt to a stop.

The ark had come to rest on a mountain.

"Can we get off the boat now, Dad?" Ham asked.

"Not yet," Noah said. "The water is still high. We have to wait for it to be safe outside."

And wait they did. Months passed. Soon they could see the tops of other mountains.

Weeks passed. Noah sent out a raven and then a dove.

Days passed. Noah sent out the dove again. It returned with an olive branch! When Noah sent out the dove for the third time, it did not return.

"Is it time to leave now, Dad?" Ham asked.

"No, son. I know it's hard to wait, but we need to trust God's timing."

Inside the ark, nothing changed. The family continued to tend the animals, spend time together and worship God.

Outside the ark, a lot was happening. God dried the ground and readied the land for Noah and his family.

One day, finally, Noah heard the words they all had been waiting to hear.

"Noah," God said. "It is time to leave the ark."

The storm was over! Life would be different. But just as God was with them on the ark, He would be with them as they took their first steps back onto land.

Stuck Together
The ark was a very big boat, but Noah and his family had to stay in it for a whole year. They had to learn to get along, solve problems together and show kindness, even when they annoyed each other. How can you show love to your family when you're stuck inside?

FOLLOWING a PROMISE

by Tim Shoemaker • based on Genesis 12 and 17

God told Abram to take a journey. It wasn't a vacation to the beach. This trip would be dangerous.

God wanted Abram to leave his friends and his nice comfy home. "Move to a new country," God said. "I will show you where to go."

Abram had to decide. Stay comfortable or take a risk. Trust God to lead him or ignore God and stay put.

Before Abram said "yes" or "no," God told Abram what would happen if he obeyed.

"I will make you into a great nation," God said.

Abram may have worried that if he left home, his family would starve. God assured him the opposite was true. Abram's family would grow stronger.

"I will bless you," God said. "And you will be a blessing to others."

Abram didn't know where he was going, but he knew God would be with him. God had a big plan. All Abram had to do was follow.

Abram didn't understand how God would bless all the nations on earth because of him, but he trusted that God always kept His promises.

Abram decided to obey. He was 75 years old when he took his wife, his cousin—and everything he owned—and started walking. His workers came with him and so did his herds of animals.

God led him to a place called Canaan.

Abram knew Canaan could be a scary place. Giants lived in Canaan, and they weren't friendly. Many of the people didn't follow God.

But Abram didn't turn back. He built an altar to God and thanked Him for sending his family to this land.

Soon the land didn't provide enough water or food for his animals. Abram didn't worry. He kept obeying God.

Abram moved his family and animals to Egypt. While he lived there, God blessed him with gold, silver and more animals. Then Abram had to move again . . . and again. In every move, he trusted God to guide him.

Abram was nearly 100 when God appeared to him again and said He was keeping His promise. Abram *would* be the father of many nations.

God changed his name to Abraham. For the rest of his life Abraham kept taking risks and trusting God.

Worth the Risk
Abram trusted and obeyed God—even when he didn't know how things would turn out. And God kept every one of His promises. Do you think God is calling you to try something new? How can you trust God more this year? Do it and see the great plans He has for you!

My Brother's Keeper

by Jacqui L. Hershberger • based on Exodus 2:1-10

"Shhhh, **Miriam,"** Mom says. "The baby is sleeping. He'll cry if you wake him!"

I sigh. I thought it would be fun to have a baby brother. It's not. Mom is always busy with him.

I know it's not her fault . . . or my brother's. Pharaoh, the mean Egyptian ruler, says all Hebrew baby boys must be thrown into the Nile River.

We've been trying to keep our baby safe, but Pharaoh's soldiers are everywhere! We can't take him outside, and he's getting too big and too noisy to hide. What will we do?

Hand me that basket," Mom says. "It's too dangerous for your baby brother to live here anymore."

She covers the basket with tar. After the tar dries, she holds my brother close. She cries and kisses him. Then she puts him in the basket.

I walk with Mom to the Nile River. She puts the basket in the tall grass at the water's edge.

"May the God of Abraham protect you," she whispers.

Mom cries as she turns to go home. I hide near the basket and watch to see what will happen.

Pharaoh's daughter comes to the river. She sees the basket. "Bring that basket to me," she tells her servant.

She pulls my brother from the basket. *WAAAAA!* he cries.

My poor baby brother. I have to do something!

I come out of my hiding place and walk up to Pharaoh's daughter. "Should I go find someone to take care of the baby?" I ask.

"Yes," she says. "Go!"

I run home and get Mom.

Pharaoh's daughter wants to keep the baby. But she needs someone to take care of him until he's bigger. She says she'll pay Mom to help raise him.

SHOULD I GO FIND SOMEONE TO TAKE CARE OF THE BABY?

YES, GO!

We take our baby home. I'm so glad we don't have to hide him anymore.

Mom is still busy with him, but I can play with him, too. And we can be noisy!

When he's big enough to go live with Pharaoh's daughter, she names him Moses. That means, "Pulled out of the water."

I'm sad to see Moses go. But I'm so glad he's alive. God must have big plans for him!

Two months had passed since the Israelites left Egypt. They'd eaten all the food they'd brought with them. Now they couldn't find any more. Their stomachs rumbled, and they began to grumble.

"In Egypt, we ate all the food we wanted," they told Moses. "But you've brought us into this desert to die!"

God had rescued them from slavery in Egypt. He'd parted the Red Sea for them.

STEP, RUMBLE, GRUMBLE

by Suzanne Gosselin • based on Exodus 16

The people seemed to have forgotten these miracles. They didn't even think that God could feed them. God gave Moses an incredible message: "I will rain down bread from heaven for you."

God gave Moses important instructions about the "manna" bread.

Step 1: Go outside each day.

Step 2: Gather enough manna for that day only.

Step 3: On the sixth day, gather twice as much.

The next morning, thin flakes covered the ground like frost.

"What's that?" the people asked.

"It's the bread the Lord has given you to eat," Moses said.

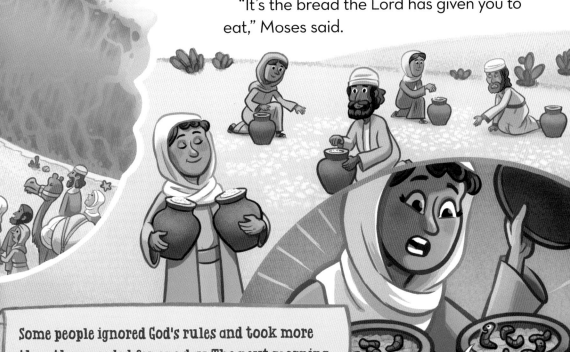

Some people ignored God's rules and took more than they needed for one day. The next morning, their manna was stinky and filled with worms!

GOOD MORNING!

STILL FRESH!

NO MORE MANNA?

On the sixth day, God gave the Israelites another message. "The Lord says tomorrow will be a day of rest," Moses said. "It will be a holy Sabbath day set apart for the Lord. So bake what you want to bake. Boil what you want to boil. Save what is left for tomorrow."

The people collected twice as much manna that day. The next morning, they lifted the lids of their pots carefully. Would the manna be stinky and filled with worms?

No! The manna was as fresh as the day before. Some people went outside to look for more, but the ground was empty.

On the seventh day, the people rested and enjoyed their manna. The heavenly bread tasted like wafers made with honey.

As they ate, the Israelites may have remembered that God rested on the seventh day after He created the world. God knew His people needed rest, too.

The Israelites ate manna for 40 years as they waited to enter the Promised Land. Every seventh day, they rested and realized that God was taking care of them.

Day of Rest
Does your family take time each week to rest and remember God's goodness? If not, give it a try. You'll be amazed at how much better you feel as you start each week!

HELPING HANDS

by Andrea Kovacs Rose • based on Exodus 17:8-16

Battle sounds echo from the valley. Moses holds his staff high over his head.

"I don't know how long I can do this," he cries.

His arms ache and tremble. His legs feel numb. Beads of sweat drip down his forehead and sting his eyes.

"Moses," Aaron says, wiping sweat off his brother's brow, "don't give up! Open your eyes and see how God is answering your prayers."

From the top of the mountain, Moses peers down at the battle. God's people, the Israelites, seem to be winning. Some Amalekite soldiers are running away.

Moses raises his staff even higher. "Help Israel, Lord!" he cries, his muscles burning with pain.

"Your staff reminds our people that God is our strength," Aaron says. "He chose you to lead us."

"Remember when God turned your staff into a snake?" Moses' friend Hur says.

"And when we were thirsty in the desert, God used your staff to provide water," Aaron adds.

"But it's been hours, and I feel so weak," Moses says with a sigh. He lowers his staff to watch the battle. Suddenly, the Amalekites start gaining ground.

"Keep that staff high," Aaron reminds Moses. "When we are weak, God is strong."

"And He gives us strength together," Hur says, placing his hand on Moses' back.

Moses nods. "With God's help, we can do all things!"

"And we can help too," Aaron says.

Aaron and Hur grab a large stone. They push it behind Moses and help him sit down.

"It feels good to sit," Moses says, "but it's still so hard to hold this staff."

"You aren't alone," Aaron says.

Aaron grabs his brother's right arm and lifts it up. Hur does the same thing with Moses' left arm. They hold Moses' arms until the battle is won.

Finally, Moses lowers his staff. "I couldn't have done it without you," he tells Aaron and Hur.

The three men build an altar so that everyone will remember how God helped the Israelites defeat their enemy.

"The Lord is my Banner," Moses proclaims. "Our victory belongs to Him!"

Stronger Together
Moses had a hard job. But God gave him a great team to help out! The Bible says God's people work best when they work together as one body.
"Each part of the body does its work. It supports the other parts. In that way, the body is joined and held together" (Ephesians 4:16).
How can you help out your friends and family?

BOLD BELIEVERS

by Kim Washburn • based on Numbers 13-14:38

THIS IS IT, GUYS.

God's people were ready to enter the Promised Land. God told Moses to choose 12 men to spy out the land.

The Israelite spies snuck into Canaan. Slowly, they crawled up a hill. Once they climbed over the ridge, they got their first glimpse of a city.

"This is it, guys," Caleb whispered, "the land God has chosen to give His people."

"I can't wait to tell Moses about this." Joshua smiled, eyeing the green fields below.

"Let's go," Palti said, standing up. "No one will see us if we go this way."

The spies quickly crossed the valley.

"So this is the land that flows with milk and honey," Caleb said.

Joshua plucked a grape from the vine. "Look at all this fruit!" He grinned, popping it in his mouth.

Caleb and Joshua walked ahead, but the 10 other Israelite spies hung back.

"Look at that wall surrounding the city," Palti whispered to Igal. "Do you think Israel has enough men to overtake it?"

Igal shook his head, eyes wide. "The city is much bigger than I thought."

LOOK AT THAT WALL.

THE CITY IS MUCH BIGGER THAN I THOUGHT.

THERE'S NO WAY WE CAN DEFEAT THESE GIANTS.

Palti scanned the horizon while they walked. Suddenly, he stopped in his tracks, his face as white as a sheep.

"Get down!" he called.

The small group of Israelites stooped under low trees. Some soldiers of Canaan stood outside the city wall.

"They're huge!" Palti said fearfully.

"There's no way we can defeat these giants," Igal said.

Caleb turned and faced the others. "You doubt we can take this land?"

"Shh," Igal begged, ducking his head. "Let's get out of here before they spot us."

"God is bigger than giants," Caleb insisted.

When the 12 spies returned to the Israelites, Joshua and Caleb believed they could take God's Promised Land.

"We can definitely do it," they said confidently. "If the Lord is pleased with us, He'll give us the victory."

But the 10 others folded their arms and shook their heads. "We can't attack those people. They are stronger than we are."

Instead of trusting God, the nation of Israel agreed with the 10 spies. They wanted to kill Joshua and Caleb.

Joshua and Caleb didn't care what the others thought. They only cared what God thought. Because of their faith, God blessed them. Joshua and Caleb were the only spies to live in the Promised Land.

Choosing to Trust

Sometimes exploring and doing new activities is fun. Other times you might feel nervous. When you feel scared, say a prayer and ask God to help you be brave. Then you can have courage like Joshua and Caleb.

KEEPING PROMISES

by Grace Kelley • based on Numbers 30:1-2

"**J**ump on!" Layla said from atop her donkey. Zeke hopped up behind his friend.

"Next stop: your tent," Layla said.

Zeke and Layla laughed and talked as they rode through the dusty Israelite camp. For years, the Israelites had camped in the wilderness. Many people complained to their leader, Moses. But Zeke's grandma stayed positive.

"Moses says that one day, we will leave this desert and live in a land flowing with milk and honey!" she often reminded him.

TWO GOATS, THREE DONKEYS AND FIVE LAMBS.

When they arrived at Zeke's tent, he jumped off.

"Your donkey is fun," Zeke said.

Layla laughed. "He's fun to ride but hard to take care of."

Zeke nodded. "Your family has so many animals."

"Two goats, three donkeys and five lambs," Layla counted. "I take care of them every morning."

Zeke felt bad for Layla.

"I can help you with the animals tomorrow morning," he said.

"Really?" Layla said. "Are you sure? You have to wake up very early."

"I'm sure." Zeke nodded. "I promise to be there."

The next morning, Zeke woke up late.

"Zeke!" his grandma called. "You need to do your morning chores."

Zeke jumped out of bed. He ate a quick breakfast and helped find firewood. After his chores, Zeke went out to play with his friends.

An hour later, Zeke saw Layla walking toward him. As she got closer, Zeke noticed she was frowning.

"You didn't help me with the animals this morning," Layla said.

Zeke's eyes grew wide. "Oh! I'm sorry. I woke up late and forgot. I can help you now."

Layla shook her head. "I already did the chores."

"OK," Zeke said, looking down at his feet.

I ALREADY DID THE CHORES.

OK.

IF A MAN GIVES HIS WORD TO DO SOMETHING, HE MUST KEEP HIS PROMISE.

Zeke felt bad. He wandered around the Israelite camp. As he walked past Moses' tent, Zeke heard him speaking to some leaders.

"Here is what the Lord commands," Moses said. "If a man gives his word to do something, he must keep his promise. He must do everything he said he would do."

Zeke felt bad again.

I broke my promise to Layla, he thought.

Zeke ran back to find Layla. "I'm sorry I didn't keep my promise," he said. "I was a bad friend today."

Layla smiled. "I forgive you."

"I'll help with the animals tomorrow," Zeke said.

"You promise?" she asked.

"I promise," he said.

I'LL HELP YOU WITH THE ANIMALS TOMORROW.

YOU PROMISE?

I PROMISE!

Promise Kept

Zeke learned to stick to his word. When we keep our promises, we show other people God's love. God always keeps His promises to us. Make sure to do the same to others.

RIGHT WRONG WORDS

by Gayleen Gardner
based on Numbers 22-24

King Balak of Moab was scared. The people of Israel were camped near his border. The king had seen how God had given the Israelites victory in battle.

"Go get Balaam, the man who listens to God," the king commanded his helpers.

Balaam was surprised when the Moabites came to his house. They offered him money to curse the Israelites.

"God already told me I cannot help King Balak," Balaam said. "I can only say what the one true God says."

The helpers brought Balaam to the king anyway.

Balaam walked up a hill where the king showed him the Israelite armies.

"Curse these people so they will go away."

"I can try, but—"

"I am the king. I say curse them," King Balak said impatiently.

Balaam opened his mouth and said to the Israelites, "May you be as strong as lions."

"What?" the king yelled. "That is not a curse! That is a blessing."

Balaam shrugged. "I can only say what God wants. God says He loves these people."

THAT IS NOT A CURSE! I AM THE KING. I SAY CURSE THEM!

The king pushed Balaam up a different hill where they could still see the people of God.

"I will pay you silver and gold! Say that these people are weak. Say they will be sick and go home."

"You could fill a palace with gold and silver, but I can only say God's words," Balaam said.

"Say it!" growled the king.

Balaam opened his mouth. "May you be as strong as a forest of tall trees."

"Stop!" bellowed the king, stomping his foot. "I told you to make them weak, not strong!"

YOU'LL BE A GREAT NATION.

King Balak tried a third time. He and Balaam climbed a tall mountain.

"Do you see how many of them are here?" the king said. "Say the words to make them go away."

Balaam tried. "God loves you. You will be a great nation," he said.

"No!" the king roared, falling to the ground. He pounded his fists on the dirt. "Why can't you do what I want?"

NO!

"Because the one true God is stronger than any king," Balaam said. "His love is forever. Nothing can separate God from His children."

Balaam got back on his donkey and went home. King Balak realized he couldn't curse people protected by God's blessing.

Always With You

God protected the Israelites because they were His people. When you accept Jesus as your Savior, you're a child of God too! You can always pray to Him for protection and peace.

"**W**e need a place to hide—fast!" the brave Israelite spies said. "Enemy soldiers are looking for us."

God wanted the wicked city of Jericho to be destroyed and for the land to belong to His people. Joshua had sent two men on a dangerous mission to spy on the walled city. But something had gone wrong. Now the men were trapped.

"We're in big trouble," the spies said.

They went to the home of Rahab—a woman whose house was built into the mighty wall of the city. Rahab let the spies inside. But somebody spotted them and raced to tell the king of Jericho.

HIDE AND SNEAK

by Tim Shoemaker • based on Joshua 2 and Joshua 6

"**H**urry," Rahab said. She led Joshua's spies to her flat roof and hid them where nobody would see them.

Suddenly, the king's soldiers banged on her door.

"Some men came to your house," the soldiers said. "They are spies. Bring them out!"

Rahab wanted to protect the spies because she knew they served Almighty God. She'd heard amazing stories of God's power.

"They were here," she said. "But they're gone."

The soldiers didn't see the spies hiding. They left and searched around the city for the spies.

"Thank you, Rahab," the spies said. "You saved our lives!"

"Please," Rahab said, "I know the Lord has given this land to you. Show me and my family kindness when your army attacks Jericho."

"We promise to keep you safe," they said. "But you must bring your family into your home and tie a red rope in your window. Then we'll know it's you."

Late that night, Rahab helped the men again. The city gates were locked. But Rahab used a rope to lower the spies from her window so they could escape.

When Joshua saw his spies, he was very thankful for what Rahab had done to help his men make it back safely.

Days later Joshua and his army came to destroy Jericho.

"Don't hurt Rahab or her family!" Joshua said. "We must rescue them."

Although the city was completely destroyed, Rahab and her family were saved. Joshua even gave Rahab's family a new place to live.

Joshua knew that sometimes the best way to say thanks is to remember the kind things people do . . . and then do something kind right back.

Saved for Good

Matthew 1 shows the family line of Jesus. Guess who's mentioned? Rahab! She was Jesus' **great-great-great-great-** (and many more greats) **great-** grandmother.

Rahab saved Joshua's spies. Then Joshua saved Rahab. And Jesus gave His life to save those who believe in Him! How can you show someone today that you're thankful for what they've done for you?

Abigail and her brother, Thomas, peeked out their window. Sisera and his army clanked by, holding weapons and riding horses. Sisera was a general from Canaan who had bullied the Israelites for 20 years.

"He's scary," Thomas said. "I don't know if we'll ever be free from Canaan."

"Look at Deborah!" Abigail pointed. "She doesn't seem afraid at all."

Their neighbor, Deborah, was a prophet and a judge. God often gave her special messages. Deborah hadn't run inside to hide from Sisera like everyone else.

"Why isn't she scared of him?" Thomas asked. "His army is so strong."

"You have to be pretty brave to be a judge like Deborah," Abigail said. "Maybe she knows something we don't."

by Amanda Jass • based on Judges 4

NO BUDGE JUDGE

When the army passed, Thomas and Abigail slipped on their sandals and ran out the door.

"Deborah, why didn't you hide?" Abigail asked.

"God has a big job for me to do," Deborah explained. "I told Barak, a leader in Israel's army, to get 10,000 men and bring them to Mount Tabor for a battle."

"And you're going to help?" Abigail shook just thinking about the battle.

"Yes, I am," Deborah said.

"Do you have a sword to protect you?" Thomas asked.

"God doesn't need swords to win battles," Deborah explained. "Even when we feel afraid, we can choose to listen to God instead of following our fear. God will protect us when we trust in Him."

LOOK AT DEBORAH! SHE DOESN'T SEEM AFRAID AT ALL.

The next morning, Thomas and Abigail watched Deborah walk toward Mount Tabor. They scrambled over to a hill where they could see from a safe distance.

Deborah, Barak and the 10,000 Israelite soldiers prepared for battle. Sisera and his army of chariots came closer.

"Get ready!" Deborah called to Barak. "This is the day that the Lord will give you victory over Sisera."

Suddenly, God brought a great storm that bogged down Sisera's chariots and confused his soldiers. The Israelites charged onto the battlefield and defeated their enemy.

As Deborah walked home, Abigail and Thomas ran to meet her.

"You did it! Sisera and his army can't bully us anymore!" they shouted.

"God did it," Deborah said with a smile. "And God used a woman to defeat Sisera, just as He said would happen."

Abigail and Thomas weren't sure what she was talking about. But they cheered along as Deborah, Barak and God's people sang praises to God. He had saved them!

Built on Trust

Deborah spent many years serving God as a judge and prophet. She learned to listen to what God wanted and to do whatever He asked, even if it was scary. She built a habit of trusting God. What habits can you build to grow closer to God?

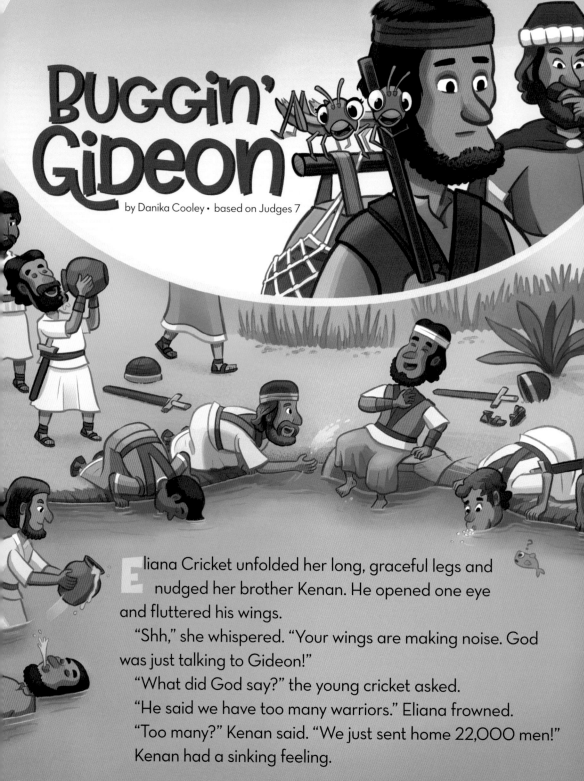

BUGGIN' GIDEON

by Danika Cooley • based on Judges 7

Eliana Cricket unfolded her long, graceful legs and nudged her brother Kenan. He opened one eye and fluttered his wings.

"Shh," she whispered. "Your wings are making noise. God was just talking to Gideon!"

"What did God say?" the young cricket asked.

"He said we have too many warriors." Eliana frowned.

"Too many?" Kenan said. "We just sent home 22,000 men!" Kenan had a sinking feeling.

When Kenan and Eliana had jumped onto Purah's backpack, they had hoped for an exciting adventure. Purah was Gideon's servant. A massive Midianite army had come to fight Israel. Now only 10,000 Israelite soldiers remained.

God spoke to Gideon again.

"There are still too many men," God said. "Take them down to the water. I will sort them out."

The stowaway crickets watched the men drink. Three hundred men kept their heads up and a hand on their swords as they cupped water with one hand and brought it to their mouths.

"With those 300 men, I will save you," God said.

Kenan gasped.

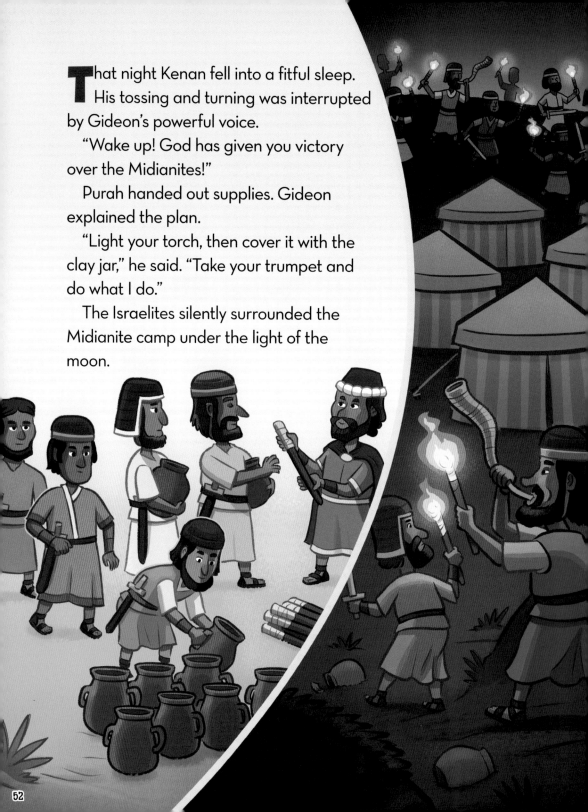

That night Kenan fell into a fitful sleep. His tossing and turning was interrupted by Gideon's powerful voice.

"Wake up! God has given you victory over the Midianites!"

Purah handed out supplies. Gideon explained the plan.

"Light your torch, then cover it with the clay jar," he said. "Take your trumpet and do what I do."

The Israelites silently surrounded the Midianite camp under the light of the moon.

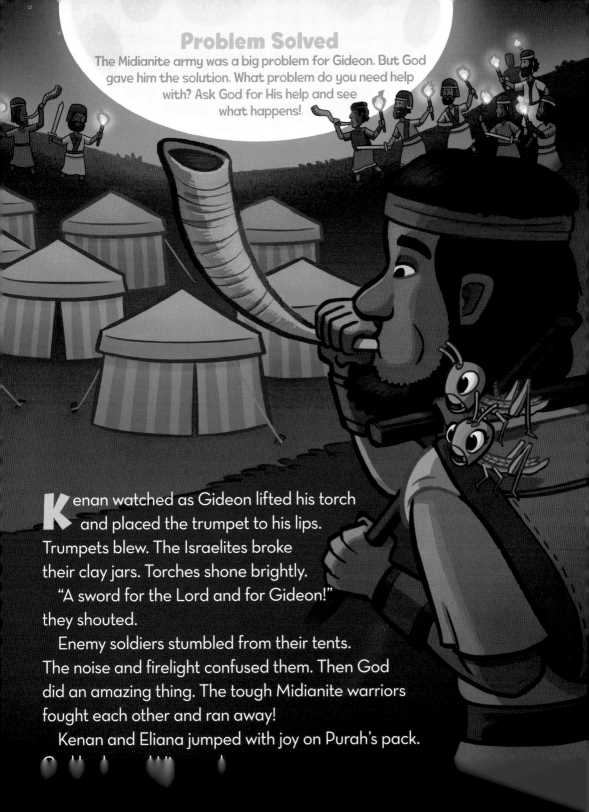

Problem Solved

The Midianite army was a big problem for Gideon. But God gave him the solution. What problem do you need help with? Ask God for His help and see what happens!

Kenan watched as Gideon lifted his torch and placed the trumpet to his lips. Trumpets blew. The Israelites broke their clay jars. Torches shone brightly.

"A sword for the Lord and for Gideon!" they shouted.

Enemy soldiers stumbled from their tents. The noise and firelight confused them. Then God did an amazing thing. The tough Midianite warriors fought each other and ran away!

Kenan and Eliana jumped with joy on Purah's pack.

Faithful Friend

by Kate Jameson • based on Ruth 1-2

Naomi was sad. But she had a plan to be happy again.

"I'm moving back home to Bethlehem," she told her daughters-in-law.

Naomi had lived in Moab with her husband and sons for 10 years. Now they had died.

"Stay here," Naomi said to Orpah and Ruth. "You were kind to my sons and to me, so may the Lord be kind to you."

"I'll miss you," Orpah said as she left.

Ruth wanted to help her mother-in-law.

"Don't try to make me leave you," Ruth said. "Where you go, I'll go. Your people will be my people. Your God will be my God."

Naomi realized she couldn't change Ruth's mind, so she let her come.

At first, life wasn't better in Bethlehem. Ruth and Naomi had no food to eat.

"Let me go out to the fields," Ruth said. "I'll pick leftover grain."

"Go ahead," Naomi said.

Ruth found a field with kind workers. They let her follow and pick up extra grain.

That day Boaz, the owner of the field, came to check on the harvest. He noticed Ruth working in the hot sun.

"Who is that young woman?" Boaz asked his top worker.

"She's from Moab," the man said. "She came back with Naomi."

Boaz walked over to Ruth.

"I hope it's OK that I'm in your field," Ruth said.

"Absolutely!" Boaz said. "Come back as much as you like."

Ruth thanked Boaz, but she looked confused. "Why are you being so kind to me?" she asked.

"I've heard about everything you have done for your mother-in-law since your husband died." Boaz smiled at Ruth. "May the Lord reward you for what you have done."

Boaz invited her to eat with his workers. After the meal, Boaz told his workers to leave extra stalks of grain for Ruth to gather.

MAY THE LORD BLESS HIM.

At the end of the day, Ruth took her harvest home. Naomi was surprised to see how much she had gathered.

"Where did you work today?" Naomi asked.

"In a field that belongs to a man named Boaz," Ruth said.

"May the Lord bless him!" Naomi said. "He is a relative of mine. The Lord is still being kind to us."

Ruth's Reward

Even though it was scary, Ruth chose to stick with Naomi during hard times. God had big plans for Ruth. She married Boaz. Then her great-grandson, David, became king of Israel. That makes Ruth the great-great-great-great- (and many more greats) grandmother of Jesus!

A MOTHER'S GIFT

by Jesse Florea • based on 1 Samuel 1-2

Hannah leaned back in her chair and let out a deep breath. Her hand was sore from sewing.

She looked at the little robe that lay across her knees.

This is the biggest one I've made, she thought. *I hope it fits. Samuel's growing so fast.*

Happy-sad tears formed in her eyes. Hannah was proud of her 7-year-old son. Samuel lived with Eli the priest in the temple. He was learning how to serve God. Hannah missed having Samuel at home.

Hannah remembered how cold she felt eight years before when she prayed to God, asking for a son. What a wild day that had been!

She and her husband were at a big celebration for God in the town of Shiloh. They went there every year to give their gifts to God. Tables were lined with delicious foods to eat and yummy things to drink. Music played, and people thanked God for all of His blessings.

But Hannah wasn't in the mood to have fun. She was sad. She had wanted to have a baby for years, but couldn't.

Hannah left the party and wandered into the temple to pray. She prayed so hard that her lips moved, but no words came out. She promised God if she had a son, then he'd serve the Lord all of his life.

Hannah didn't know it, but Eli saw her praying. Eli could tell she was praying with all of her heart.

"May the God of Israel give you what you have asked Him," Eli said to her.

Hannah decided if God gave her a son, she would have Eli teach him about God.

A year later Hannah gave birth to a son and named him Samuel.

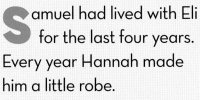amuel had lived with Eli for the last four years. Every year Hannah made him a little robe.

"Now for the finishing touch," she said.

Hannah always wrote a special note to her firstborn son. She reached for some paper and started to write:

My dearest Samuel,
I love you very much and think about you always.
It's clear that God is going to use you to do great things. Be patient as you wait for God to lead you. Always seek after the Lord. He knows everything, and He'll give you strength to follow Him.
You'll always be my gift from God.
Your loving mother,
Hannah

Draw a picture or write a note to your mom to let her know how much you love her.

AN ARMY OF TWO

by Tim Shoemaker • based on 1 Samuel 13:16-14:23

"Let's go to the Philistine camp," Jonathan said to me. (I'm an armor-bearer. I work for Jonathan, the son of King Saul.)

Just the two of us against a huge enemy army? I thought. *We'll be completely outnumbered!*

The Philistine army was huge. They camped nearby, raiding Israelite towns while King Saul and his tiny army hid.

Jonathan couldn't stand waiting around. He wanted to help. So did I. He stood and motioned for me to follow him.

I slung Jonathan's shield over my back and grabbed his sword and spear. Quietly, we snuck out and walked toward the high cliffs.

My job was to follow Jonathan into battle and carry his extra weapons. That was easy these days. Out of the whole Israelite army, only King Saul and Jonathan had a sword and spear. Our army had to fight the Philistines with sticks and stones.

"It doesn't matter how many men are in their army or how few are in ours," Jonathan said. "Nothing can stop the Lord from saving us."

Although I was scared, I knew Jonathan was right.

"Let's do this," I said. "I'm with you heart and soul."

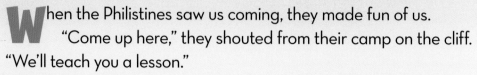

When the Philistines saw us coming, they made fun of us.

"Come up here," they shouted from their camp on the cliff. "We'll teach you a lesson."

Jonathan glanced back at me. "The Lord has handed over our enemies to us," he said. "Ready?"

I thumped my chest and nodded. Using our hands and feet, we climbed to the waiting Philistines. I handed Jonathan his sword, and he headed straight for the army.

Enemy soldiers fell in front of Jonathan because God fought for us. They shook as God sent a panic throughout the Philistine army.

Courageous Faith

Jonathan and his armor-bearer were outnumbered and had only one spear and one sword. But they had a much better weapon: faith. They believed God would keep them safe and help them win. How can you show your faith in God?

he Philistines ran around in confusion.
In their fear, they fought each other! King Saul and the Israelite army saw what was happening. They jumped up and helped chase the Philistines away. Israel was rescued.

When Jonathan saw the Philistines running away, he smiled at me. God had rewarded our courage.

When we go with God, I thought, *we're never outnumbered!*

FIVE SMOOTH STONES

by Rachel Pfeiffer • based on 1 Samuel 17:1-50

David looked at the new shepherd. "My brothers are fighting with King Saul's army," he said. "I need to bring them food, so you must watch the sheep."

"*Baaa,*" Sam the sheep said.

He always stayed close to David. Sam wasn't happy his shepherd was leaving.

Who will protect David if I'm not around? Sam thought.

"I'll be back before you know it," David said as he left.

Sam watched the new shepherd chase Fluffy. She was always wandering off.

Now's my chance, Sam thought.

With the shepherd distracted, Sam dashed over the hill.

Sam tried hard to stay hidden behind trees and bushes as he followed his shepherd. But as they approached the Israelite camp, he accidently stepped on a twig. *Snap!*

David spun around and saw Sam. "Sam, I told you to stay behind!"

"*Baaa*," Sam said.

David sighed. "Stay close to me so you don't get lost."

The two made their way through the camp. On the battlefield, a Philistine soldier shouted. He was bigger than any man that Sam had ever seen.

"Choose one of your men. Have him come down and face me," the giant said. "If he is able to defeat me, we will serve you. But if I win, you will serve us."

"Who is that?" David asked.

"That's Goliath," one man said. "We're too afraid to fight him."

David frowned. "Come on, Sam. We need to talk to the king."

I'LL FIGHT GOLIATH.

YOU ARE TOO YOUNG.

"I'll fight Goliath," David said.

"You are too young," King Saul replied. "Goliath has been a warrior since he was a boy."

David stood taller. "With God's help, I've defeated lions and bears that tried to eat my father's sheep. I know the Lord will save me from Goliath too."

King Saul sighed. "Go. And may the Lord be with you."

Sam followed David down to the stream.

"Don't look so worried, Sam," David said. "God is with me. Now help me find good stones for my sling."

Sam nudged rocks toward David. In no time they had five smooth stones.

David put the stones in his bag. "Now I'm ready to face Goliath."

avid walked onto the battlefield. "This day the Lord will give me the victory over you," David announced to Goliath. "Today the whole world will know there is a God in Israel."

"*Baaa,*" Sam said as he hung back at the Israelite camp. He tried to sound brave, but his voice shook.

Goliath moved toward David. David ran at Goliath. He pulled one of the stones out of his bag. David swung his sling and flung the stone at Goliath.

Whack! The stone hit Goliath. The giant fell to the ground. The Israelites cheered.

Sam jumped and pranced. God protected David and gave him victory!

Full of Power

David believed in God's power. God helped him do what everyone thought was impossible. How can you be bold in your faith and do something awesome this month?

MAKING PEACE

by Suzanne Gosselin • based on 1 Samuel 25:1-35

In the Desert of Maon lived a rich man named Nabal. Nabal had many sheep, goats and servants. But Nabal was rude and mean. He was known for treating others badly.

David and his army camped near Nabal's sheep. They never stole anything. Nabal's shepherds stayed near David's soldiers for protection.

One day, David and his men were hungry. David sent 10 men to ask Nabal for food. David's men had been kind to Nabal's shepherds. David thought Nabal would be kind to them and give them something to eat.

David's men told Nabal how the army had protected Nabal's sheep and shepherds. They asked him for food.

Nabal responded rudely. "I don't know this David! Why should I give you the food that I worked so hard to grow? I won't share anything."

When David's men returned with nothing, David was very angry. He decided to attack Nabal for his disrespect.

While David organized his army, one of Nabal's servants rushed to his wife, Abigail. Abigail was smart and beautiful. The servant knew David would be angry at Nabal's lack of kindness.

"David's men were good to us," the servant said. "They treated us well. Nabal was evil in how he treated David. Now disaster is hanging over our whole household. What can we do?"

Abigail quickly made a plan. She packed loaves of bread, lots of meat, large containers of roasted grain, and hundreds of cakes made of figs and raisins. She loaded everything on donkeys and went to meet David.

Smart Thinking

Abigail's quick thinking saved many lives. When you face a problem, God can help you think of a creative solution. James 1:5 says, "If any of you needs wisdom, you should ask God for it. He will give it to you." God's answers are always best. He will help you do what's right!

When Abigail saw David, she climbed off her donkey and bowed down.

"Please forgive your wicked servant, Nabal," she begged. "Accept this gift of food for your men."

Abigail reminded David that he served the Lord. She asked him to live in peace with her household.

David knew Abigail was right. He thanked her for stopping his attack.

"May the Lord bless you for what you have done," David said. "You have shown good sense and saved the day."

David accepted her gift and told her to return home in peace.

The Widow

by Beth Goehringer • based on 1 Kings 17:8-16

A tear rolled down the widow's cheek.

"God, where are You?" she cried. "My husband died. Now the rains are gone. The land is so dry that there's no food."

Tears ran down her face. "My son and I will die soon. Lord, we really need Your help."

The widow stared at the little flour she had left. Then she swirled the bit of oil that remained in the jug. Maybe she had enough for one more barley cake.

The widow sighed and slung a basket over her arm. She needed to gather firewood— just enough to cook their last meal.

Stooping, the widow picked up sticks and put them in her basket. Tears blurred her vision. She reached for a small log, but it moved.

That's not a log, she realized. *It's a man's foot!*

The widow looked up. The man smiled.

It's the prophet Elijah, she thought.

She'd seen him before. She'd also heard amazing stories about miracles God did through him.

"Would you bring me a little water?" he said. "I need a drink."

The widow hurried to the well.

"Please bring me a piece of bread, too," he called.

"I don't have any bread," she said, pointing at her basket. "I'm gathering sticks to make a fire, so I can bake one last meal for myself and my son."

Elijah looked into her sad eyes. "Don't be afraid," he said. "Go home and make a small loaf of bread for me. Then make some for yourself and your son. The Lord says, 'You will have flour and oil until the day the Lord sends rain on the land.'"

The widow went home.

If I do what Elijah said, there will be nothing left, she thought. *But I need to trust what the Lord said.*

She baked some bread for Elijah. Then she looked in the jar. It had flour in it. Her oil jug seemed to have even more oil than before!

The widow cried tears of joy. She invited Elijah to stay with her.

Every day, they had exactly enough to eat. The flour and oil never ran out, just as the Lord had promised.

Great Provider

"He gives those who are thirsty all the water they want. He gives those who are hungry all the good food they can eat."

—Psalm 107:9

saving the PROPHETS

by Amanda Jass • based on 1 Kings 17:1-5 and 18:1-16

Obadiah had a big job. He was in charge of King Ahab's entire palace! He was always one of the first people to hear about new plans for the nation of Israel.

King Ahab wasn't a good ruler. Queen Jezebel was even worse. The king and queen worshiped idols—not the one true God. They wanted the Israelites to worship their false gods too.

Idol worship made God angry. Because King Ahab and Queen Jezebel disobeyed God, the prophet Elijah came to the palace.

"God will stop the rain," he said.

That made King Ahab and Queen Jezebel angry. Elijah left the palace and went into hiding.

Three years later, it still hadn't rained in Israel.

Queen Jezebel was very upset. "We should gather up all the prophets," she said. "And then get rid of them."

Obadiah couldn't believe his ears. The prophets got messages from God and told the people God's words, just like the prophet Elijah had.

Obadiah loved God. He had served God since he was a child. He didn't want to see the prophets killed.

I can't let this happen, Obadiah thought.

He knew that God wanted him to love and care for others. But if he got caught helping God's prophets, he'd be in big trouble.

Obadiah decided to help the prophets hide.
    He found 100 prophets. Then Obadiah found two big, dark
caves outside the city. All the prophets would fit inside. Obadiah
visited them often, bringing them food and water.
    God watched over Obadiah as he cared for the prophets.

One day, Elijah came to Obadiah.

"I have a message for King Ahab from God," Elijah said. "Please tell him I want to talk to him."

"I can't do that!" Obadiah said. "If the king finds out I've talked to you, I'll get in trouble!"

"God will keep us safe," Elijah said. "I will speak to Ahab today."

I don't want to get in trouble, Obadiah thought. *But maybe Elijah can convince King Ahab to listen to God.*

"All right," Obadiah said. "I'll help you."

GOD WILL KEEP US SAFE.

A Big Risk

Thanks to Obadiah, Elijah showed King Ahab that God was the only One to be worshiped. God sent rain to end the drought, and Obadiah was happy that he did the right thing. Have you ever had to make a sacrifice to serve God?

Jethro liked to sing as he cooked.
"Boil, boil, stir the pot.
Soon the water will be hot."
Jethro's stomach growled. He looked in the pot.
What am I going to do? Jethro wondered. *I only have a pot of water.*
Hot water was not a fitting meal for God's prophet Elisha. But a famine had spread across the land. No matter how hard everyone worked, they had little food.
And today Jethro was helping Elisha's servant, Gehazi, cook a meal for the prophet and some students.
Grrrrrr, Jethro's stomach growled again.

TO → PERFECTION

by Dr. Mary Manz Simon • based on 2 Kings 4:38-41

Jethro added a log to the fire. He looked around at what had once been a lush olive grove. Now, the twisted branches were almost bare.

Soon, Elisha will finish teaching for the day, Jethro thought. *Everyone will want to eat.*

Just then Jethro's friend, Gad, ran up to him.

"What's for supper?" Gad asked, walking over to the pot. "Elisha sent me to help get it ready."

"We don't have anything for the stew." Jethro shook his head.

Jethro and Gad left the pot and trudged among the brown fields. They scattered to hunt for anything edible. Jethro looked in sandy soil where grain had once grown tall. Gad hunted for grapes that might have fallen between rocks.

"Over here!" Gad called.

Jethro ran to his friend. Gad had found a plant almost hidden in the rocky earth. Tiny gourds hung limply on the vine. The plant didn't look familiar, but they eagerly gathered each precious gourd. They ran back to the camp where the other students looked hopelessly at the empty pot.

"Look! See what we found," Jethro called.

Eager and excited, the students sang as they watched Gad slice the small gourds into the boiling pot.

"Can you smell the bubbling stew? We'll have food for me and you."

Elisha joined the happy students. After a day of learning about God, everyone would eat well. But when Gad tasted the stew, he spit it on the ground. Alarmed, Jethro took a small taste and choked.

A third student smelled the stew and gagged. "The gourds in the stew are poisonous!"

Everyone glared at Jethro and Gad.

Elisha calmly walked to the pot and smiled at Jethro. "Bring me some flour," he said.

Jethro fetched some flour and handed it to him. Tossing the flour into the pot, the prophet sang.

"Let's all eat a bowl of stew.

God provides; we know that's true."

Gad tasted the stew again and grinned. "It's delicious!"

Everyone cheered.

Thank You, God, Jethro prayed.

Perfect Plan
What do you do when things don't go as planned? God doesn't want you to be angry or say mean words when plans go wrong. Instead, work with your family or friends to encourage each other and fix the situation.

MIRACLE AT

by Tim Shoemaker • based on 2 Kings 6:1-7

Sarah raced down the path to the Jordan River.

Her siblings didn't like washing clothes, but Sarah enjoyed the chore. She looked forward to sitting next to the peaceful waters and singing her favorite songs.

Sarah smiled as she hopped over a rock. Carefully, she carried the basket to the river. As Sarah neared the river's edge, she heard voices along the bank.

"Here's a good spot for us to build a place to live," a man's voice called.

Thwack, thwack, thwack. A tree fell with a **CRASH**.

Sarah screamed and jumped in surprise.

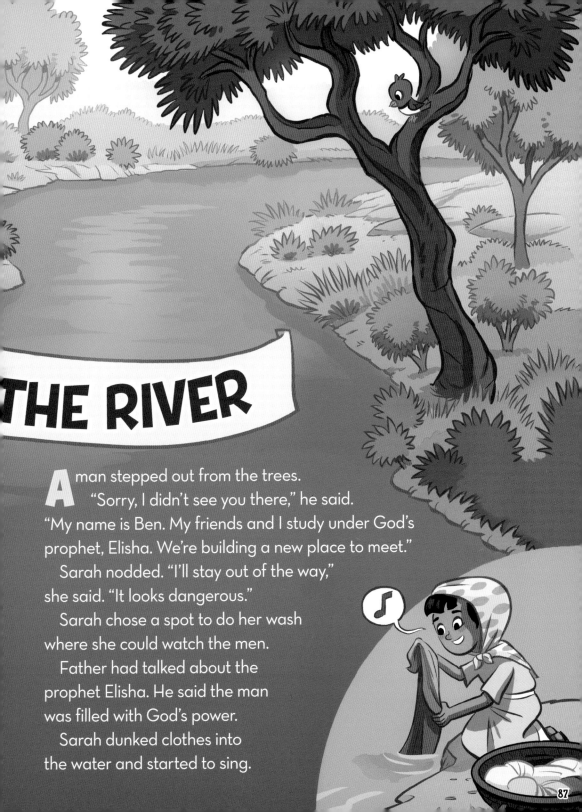

THE RIVER

A man stepped out from the trees.

"Sorry, I didn't see you there," he said. "My name is Ben. My friends and I study under God's prophet, Elisha. We're building a new place to meet."

Sarah nodded. "I'll stay out of the way," she said. "It looks dangerous."

Sarah chose a spot to do her wash where she could watch the men.

Father had talked about the prophet Elisha. He said the man was filled with God's power.

Sarah dunked clothes into the water and started to sing.

The men's sharp axes flashed in the sun as they worked. Suddenly, Ben swung his ax so hard that the iron ax-head flew off.

Splash! The heavy blade disappeared below the murky waters of the Jordan River.

"Oh no!" Ben cried. He turned to an older man who had come to watch the work. "Teacher, this ax was borrowed."

So that's the prophet Elisha, Sarah thought. *He doesn't look powerful.*

"I can't pay to replace the ax," Ben continued. "I'll have to leave and work for the owner until my debt is repaid."

Sarah frowned. *It's sad he'll have to leave his friends,* she thought.

Where did it fall?" Elisha asked.

Ben pointed to a spot. Elisha threw a stick into the water where the ax disappeared. Out of nowhere, the ax bobbed to the surface!

"Take it out," Elisha said.

Ben gratefully grasped the ax and praised God.

Sarah gasped. She left her wash and raced back up the path.

"Mother!" Sarah called as she ran into her house. "You'll never believe what happened at the river!"

The Impossible

An iron ax can't float. But with God's power, Elisha made an impossible miracle happen. God is the same today as He was in the days of Elisha. He won't always fix our problems with a miracle. But He is always faithful to help us. The next time you face a big problem, pray to Him. No problem is too big for God!

Invisible Army

by Mike Nappa • based on 2 Kings 6:8-23

When I started working for the prophet Elisha, I was nervous. But it's been exciting so far, almost like working for a spy!

Our country, Israel, is at war. God keeps telling Elisha where the enemy plans to strike next. Elisha tells our army, so they're ready and waiting when the enemy arrives.

The enemy king must wonder how we know his plans.

Uh-oh. He found out. And now he's planning to capture Elisha!

"**D**on't be scared," I say to myself. "Don't be afraid, nuh-uh-no-way! Just be brave . . . and . . . AAHHH! OK, I admit it. My boss, Elisha, may be God's prophet, but I'm terrified! I think I'll run and hide."

"id I hear my name?" Elisha asks, walking into the room. "What's the problem?"

I point at the massive army outside.

"Aram's army has come to capture you," I say. "No doubt they'll take me prisoner, too. I'm thinking we should surrender. Or hide in large clay jars. Or . . ."

"Don't be afraid," Elisha says. "Those who are with us are more than those who are with them."

What is he talking about? I wonder.

"**O**pen my servant's eyes, LORD," Elisha prays, "so he may see." I look out the window and see a huge army of heavenly warriors riding in chariots of fire! The invisible army is even bigger than the visible one. No wonder Elisha's not afraid!

Higher Help

Sometimes bad things come out of nowhere—like an army of enemies! But God is never surprised when bad things happen.

Like Elisha, we can trust God and show kindness to our enemies. God can help us through anything!

The enemy soldiers move to capture us.

"Please strike them with blindness," Elisha prays.

God blinds our enemies. Elisha leads them to the king of Israel. When God gives the Aram army back its sight, the soldiers open their eyes to see Israel's army all around them.

Our king wants to kill them, but Elisha says to feed them instead. The enemy army eats a great feast and heads home. They never invade Israel again.

LAW OF THE LAND

by Jesse Florea • based on 2 Kings 22-23:25

When Josiah became king of Judah, the people didn't care about God. The Lord's temple was falling apart. God's Word was nowhere to be found.

Josiah's father and grandfather had been terrible kings. They worshiped evil idols and led the people away from the one true God.

Josiah was 8 years old when the crown was put on his head. He was young, but he learned to be wise. He didn't follow past wicked kings. He followed God.

By the time Josiah turned 20, he destroyed many altars to false gods.

Smash. Crack. Slam! Down came buildings and shrines. These evil places encouraged people to worship sun and moon gods. Josiah wanted the people to worship the Creator of the sun, moon, earth . . . and universe!

He found skilled workers to rebuild the Lord's temple. As workers cleaned out the temple, Hilkiah the priest found the Book of the Law.

Hilkiah read the scrolls to Josiah. When the king heard God's Word, he tore his clothes in shame because the people had drifted so far away from God.

Josiah called all the people to the temple. Rich and poor, old and young, everyone came to hear the king. He stood next to a large pillar and read all of God's Word.

Josiah promised to obey God's laws and commands. The people agreed to follow God's laws too.

The people changed their evil habits. They stopped following false gods.

Josiah kept tearing down evil altars. **Boom. Smush. Blam!** He cleaned up the temple and made it a holy place again.

Then the king gave an order. "Let's celebrate to honor the Lord our God," he said. "We will do what is written in the Book of the Law."

The king threw a huge feast. Josiah was happy. The people were happy too because they knew and followed God's rules.

What Is Right

Josiah used all his might to do what was pleasing in God's sight. When he heard God's law, he knew these rules would give him freedom and success. What rules do you follow to have a good, safe life?

RICH BEYOND COMPARE

by Kate Jameson • based on 2 Chronicles 1:1-12

Solomon had been crowned king of Israel. His father, David, was a great king. Solomon wanted to be a great king too. Solomon decided to spend time talking to the people of Israel. He spoke to commanders in the army. He spoke to judges. He spoke to family leaders. He wanted to know the people and what they needed. By talking to them, he hoped to build good relationships.

ASK FOR ANYTHING YOU WANT ME TO GIVE YOU!

Solomon knew that he needed to have a good relationship with God too. He prayed in the tabernacle and asked God for advice. He asked other people to pray too.

One night, God spoke to Solomon. "Ask for anything you want me to give you," God said.

Anything? Solomon thought. *I have a big choice to make.*

Solomon thought and thought about what to ask for.
He could ask for money and be richer than anyone in the
world. Strong armies could defend Israel from its enemies. If God
made everyone love and respect him, being king would be easier.
Gifts like horses and fancy houses would be lots of fun.

But Solomon knew what he needed most.

"You were very kind to my father David," Solomon said to God.
"You have made me king. Give me wisdom and knowledge.
Without Your help, who would be able to rule this great nation
of Yours?"

God was very happy with Solomon. "You want to be able to rule my people wisely," He said. "So wisdom and knowledge will be given to you. I will also give you wealth, possessions and honor. You will have more than any king before you ever had."

Solomon was shocked. God not only made him a wise king, but God promised him a lot more!

A Big Gift
Instead of asking for money, fame or an unlimited supply of candy, Solomon asked for wisdom. He knew that to be a good and fair king, he needed to be wise. God rewarded Solomon's selfless request by making him wise *and* rich *and* famous! How can you use your gifts to help other people?

WHAT'S THAT?

LET'S GO SEE.

Bang! Bam! Boom!

Ami and Alex looked around their cozy den. Their ears twitched as the banging continued.

"What's that?" Ami asked her brother.

Alex tilted his head. "Let's go see."

The two foxes scurried up a dirt slope. They slid through some rocks, just outside the city of Jerusalem.

"Look! God's people are trying to rebuild the broken wall," Alex said. "Even the leaders like Nehemiah are helping out."

"But how can they build a wall around the whole city?" Ami frowned. "It's too big!"

BIG JOB IN JERUSALEM

by Kathleen Wilcox • based on Nehemiah 4 and 6:15

The next day the curious foxes stood by the road as two men rode into Jerusalem.

"Ah-choo!" Alex wrinkled his nose as dust filled the air.

"Cover your mouth," Ami whispered.

"You people are too weak to build a wall!" one man yelled.

"If a fox jumps on it, it will crumble." The other man laughed.

"Sure, blame us," Alex said, rolling his eyes.

The Israelites tried to ignore these two bullies. The workers kept stacking stones on the wall.

Each morning, Ami and Alex hurried out to watch.

"Look, that girl is helping her dad," Alex said. "Other kids are working too."

"Every stone helps." Ami nodded. "Even little ones."

O ne day, people rushed into Jerusalem.
"You're in danger," they warned. "Your enemies will attack anyone building the wall."

The people were tired and afraid. Nehemiah stayed calm. He prayed and called everyone together. Ami and Alex hid in a nearby bush to listen.

"Don't be afraid!" Nehemiah encouraged. "Remember, God is great and powerful."

Everyone nodded and went back to work. Some kept building the walls and others kept watch for danger.

Days later, Ami and Alex heard cheering instead of hammering. They hopped out of their den. The wall was finished! All the people were praising God.

"It's so big!" Ami said. She followed Alex up the wall stairs.

"Let's play tag," Alex said. "Try to catch me!" He dashed away.

Ami chased and tagged his bushy tail. "You're it!" She spun around and ran like the wind.

"Look, Dad," a girl said. "Two foxes are on the wall, and it's still standing strong!"

Brave Builders

Through prayer and hard work, the Israelites rebuilt Jerusalem's wall in only 52 days! Even their enemies knew God made it possible. When we work together and ask God for help, we can do big things too!

THE BRAVE QUEEN

by Kate Jameson • based on the book of Esther

"We're moving?" Esther asked. "But why? I like it here."

Mordecai, Esther's adopted father, smiled. "I have a new job at the palace. We need to be closer."

Esther sighed. "I just wish we didn't have to leave."

"I know change is hard," Mordecai said. "But God puts us where we need to be. You'll see."

Esther and Mordecai settled into their new home. Slowly, Esther got used to the new city.

"It's nice here," Esther admitted one night. "Even though I miss my old friends, I'm glad we moved."

A short time later, an announcement went out to the entire Persian kingdom. The king was looking for a new queen! Many young women would be chosen to move to the palace so the king could pick a queen.

Esther was taken to the king's palace. But she wasn't excited.

"I don't like change," she told Mordecai while she packed. "I want to stay here with you."

"I know," Mordecai said. "Trust that God has a plan."

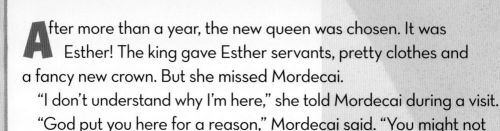

After more than a year, the new queen was chosen. It was Esther! The king gave Esther servants, pretty clothes and a fancy new crown. But she missed Mordecai.

"I don't understand why I'm here," she told Mordecai during a visit.

"God put you here for a reason," Mordecai said. "You might not know what it is right now, but trust Him."

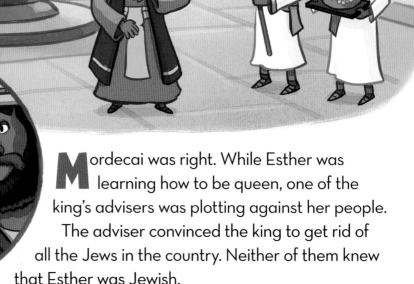

Mordecai was right. While Esther was learning how to be queen, one of the king's advisers was plotting against her people. The adviser convinced the king to get rid of all the Jews in the country. Neither of them knew that Esther was Jewish.

"Maybe this is why God brought you here," Mordecai told Esther when he learned about the evil plan. "It won't be easy, but you can help save our people."

Esther nodded. She would trust God. She would be brave and make her own plan. She invited the king and the bad adviser to dinner. Through her kindness and honesty, she convinced the king to change his mind and not hurt the Jews. Her people were saved!

Trust During Change
Many changes turned Esther's life upside down. She trusted in God and ended up saving her people. It can be hard to deal with changes, big or small. But God has a purpose for them all.

TRUST NO MatteR WHat

by Hannah Dodd
based on the book of Job

"Father, we're having a party," Job's daughter said. "Will you come?"

Job had seven sons and three daughters. They loved to spend time together.

"Not today, dear," Job said.

That night, a messenger came to Job.

"All of your sheep, camels, oxen and donkeys are gone," he said.

"Oh no!" Job exclaimed.

More messengers came with bad news. The last one told Job that his children were gone.

Job was sad and scared. But he trusted in God's love. "Lord, You give and take away. Thank You for the things I still have. I will trust You."

Meanwhile, God was talking to Satan.

"You think Job will love You no matter what?" Satan said. "Ha! I'll show You."

"Go ahead and try, Satan," God replied. "I know Job better than anyone else. He will never stop trusting Me."

"If I take away everything he cares about, surely he will stop believing in You," Satan said.

After Satan wiped out Job's family and animals, he made Job very sick.

Job didn't know why everything in his life was going wrong. People thought Job had done something bad and was being punished. But Job always honored God. God knew Job would stay strong. Even though lots of things went wrong, Job knew God loved him. And that was all he needed.

No matter how hard Satan tried, Job's faith stayed strong. Satan was defeated.

"Fine, I give up," Satan said to God.

Then God did a marvelous thing. He gave Job back all the things he lost . . . and then doubled it! He even had more children.

"Wow, what a gift!" Job said. "Thank You, Lord. I know I can always trust You."

Always Trust
Sometimes bad things happen in life. When things go wrong, we should act like Job and trust God. God always loves us. His love never stops . . . even during hard times!

by Carol Johnson • based on Jeremiah 36

TRY, TRY Again

God loved His people, but they were not following Him. He told Jeremiah to warn the Israelites that another nation would destroy them if they did not change their wicked ways. The people would not listen.

God gave them another chance to hear His words. God told Jeremiah to write down a message.

Jeremiah and his friend Baruch loved God's words. They wanted the people to love them too. They worked for a whole year, writing God's message on a scroll. Finally, they were finished!

Jeremiah sent Baruch to the temple to read God's words to the people.

"Maybe they will listen and follow God," Jeremiah said.

Baruch carried the scroll to the temple. He stood near a gate where many people could hear. With a loud, strong voice, Baruch read the scroll. People stopped to listen.

But one important group of people was missing—the rulers. They were in the palace.

A young man heard Baruch and ran to the palace. "You'll never guess what's happening in the temple!" he said.

YOU'LL NEVER GUESS WHAT'S HAPPENING IN THE TEMPLE!

115

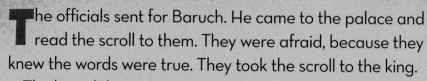

The officials sent for Baruch. He came to the palace and read the scroll to them. They were afraid, because they knew the words were true. They took the scroll to the king.

The king did not want to hear the truth of God's words. He stopped his officials from reading it. The king cut off sections of the scroll and threw them into a fire.

Some of the officials tried to stop him. "Please! No! Those are the words of God. You must show respect!"

But the king did not listen. He did not fear God's words. He burned the entire scroll.

"I don't believe God's warning!" the king said. "Go arrest Jeremiah and Baruch."

God hid Jeremiah and Baruch. The king's men searched but could not find them.

RRRRIP!

Jeremiah and Baruch rewrote God's words on a new scroll.

While Jeremiah and Baruch were safe, the king was not. He was replaced with a new king. And because the people did not honor God's words, another nation came and took them captive.

Living Words

God told Jeremiah and Baruch to share His words. Even when their hard work was burned up, they didn't give up. They wrote a new scroll. Ask God to help you love, honor and share His words—just like Jeremiah and Baruch did!

Writing on the Wall

by Jacqui Hershberger • based on Daniel 5

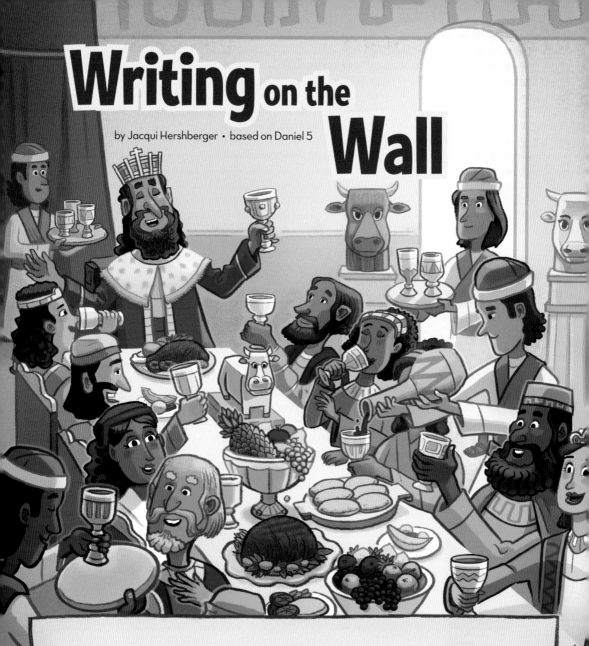

King Belshazzar had a big feast and invited 1,000 of his powerful friends. He asked his servants to bring in gold and silver cups. The cups had been taken from God's temple in Jerusalem. All the people drank from the stolen cups and praised their false gods.

Suddenly, a hand appeared and wrote on the palace wall. Belshazzar stared. His knees began to knock together. Nobody could read the writing, so he asked the wisest people in his kingdom to come read it. They didn't understand it, either.

MENE MENE
TEKEL
PARSIN

The queen said they should send for Daniel, a wise man who had served King Nebuchadnezzar.

MENE MENE TEKEL PARSIN

Daniel read the words and told Belshazzar that he had become very proud. He reminded him that Nebuchadnezzar once lived like a wild animal until he honored God.

"Even though you know what happened to him," Daniel said, "you still use cups from the Lord's temple and praise your pretend gods, instead of the one true God."

Daniel told Belshazzar that God was sending him a message. Because he didn't honor God, his kingdom would be given to other nations.

That very night, Darius the Mede was crowned the new king, just as God had said.

Watch and Learn

Have you ever learned how to *not* get into trouble by seeing what happened to someone else who did? Why is it important to avoid following someone else's bad actions?

LION TAMER

by Linda Gondosch • based on Daniel 6:1-27

King Darius of Babylon thought Daniel was his best worker. He planned to put Daniel in charge of his entire kingdom. The other government officials were jealous.

"Let's get Daniel in trouble," one of them said. "If he breaks the law, he can't be in charge."

But there was a problem with their plan. Daniel never broke any laws.

The officials decided they needed to trick the king. They visited King Darius and said, "We think everyone should pray to you. If anyone prays to any other man or god, he should be fed to the lions."

"An excellent idea!" the king said. "I like being worshiped."

GREAT IDEA!

Daniel loved God. Daniel had been taken from Jerusalem as a child. But he still prayed to the God of Israel every day. He liked King Darius, but Daniel trusted in God more.

Even in great danger where I might end up looking a lion in the eye, Daniel thought, *I will not pray to King Darius—even if I die.*

Daniel knelt by his window.

"I thank You, God, for all things, and I humbly ask for Your help," he prayed.

"Look!" shouted an official who was spying on Daniel. "He is praying to his God."

The officials ran to the palace. "O great king, we have terrible news," they said. "We saw Daniel praying to his God. He disobeyed your law. Throw him to the lions!"

The king frowned.

"I wish I'd never made that law," he said. But the king knew he could not change his orders.

"Throw Daniel into the lions' den," King Darius said sadly.

As Daniel was led to the den, he heard ferocious growls. The lions opened their powerful jaws and ROARED!

"I hope your God rescues you," the king said.

God can rescue me from anything, Daniel thought. *My faith is in Him.*

Daniel bravely went into the lions' den. Then the king's men put a heavy rock over the entrance.

That evening the king could not sleep. All he could think about was Daniel in a cold, dark den filled with hungry lions.

The next morning King Darius ran to the lions' den.

"Daniel, Daniel, can you hear me?" he yelled.

"I am alive, good king," Daniel replied. "God sent an angel to shut the mouths of the lions. Praise be to God!"

When King Darius saw Daniel, he was amazed. Daniel didn't even have a scratch on him.

"From this day on," the joyful king ordered, "we will respect God. Daniel's God truly rescues and saves. He even saved Daniel from the lions!"

Lionhearted

When have you shown bravery to follow God? Maybe you prayed before eating lunch or brought your Bible to school. Think of ways that you can show others that you love God.

by Rachel Pfeiffer • based on Jonah 1-3

FISH TALE

Jonah was a prophet. Prophets listened to messages from God. Then they told the people what God said.

"Go to the great city of Nineveh," God told Jonah. "Preach against it. The sins of its people have come to my attention."

The people in Nineveh are mean, Jonah thought. *I don't want to help them.*

Instead of doing what God told him, Jonah found a ship sailing away from Nineveh. *If I go the other way, God can't make me preach to the Ninevites,* Jonah thought.

He boarded the ship and found a place to sleep.

oon the captain shook Jonah awake.

What's happening? Jonah wondered. He followed the captain onto the deck. Before he could say anything, pouring rain stung his eyes. A mighty storm was about to sink the ship.

The sailors gathered on the deck. "Someone is to blame for getting us into this trouble."

They all looked at Jonah.

"I worship the Lord," Jonah said. "God told me to preach to the Ninevites, but I ran away. Throw me into the sea, then it will become calm."

The sailors tried to row back to land, but it was no use. They tossed Jonah into the crashing waves.

onah sank into the water. Suddenly, he felt the mouth of a giant
fish around him.

I'm being eaten! he thought.

Jonah slid into the fish's belly.

This isn't funny, God, Jonah thought. He sat in the stinky, smelly
belly of the fish for three days. Then he started to pray. *God, I'm
sorry I ran away from You. Please forgive me and save me from this
giant fish.*

Jonah felt himself sliding back the way he'd come. He burst out
onto dry land. Jonah coughed and squinted in the sunlight.

"Go to the great city of Nineveh," God said. "Announce to the
people the message I give you."

"OK," Jonah answered.

Jonah walked into the city. "In 40 days, Nineveh will be destroyed!" he announced.

The Ninevites believed him. From the king to the lowly workers, everyone asked God to forgive them. They stopped doing evil things.

God saw how sorry the people were. He decided not to destroy the city.

Many people were saved because Jonah finally obeyed God.

Awesome Adventure

Do you ever think following God is too hard or too boring? God always knows what's best for you. The plans He has for you probably don't involve being swallowed by a giant fish. But living your life for God is an awesome adventure!

Wait for It

by Hannah Dodd
based on the book of Habakkuk

Habakkuk the prophet walked along a dirt road to his home. He opened up the door, set down his water jug and plopped onto his bed.

Habakkuk's job was to give important messages from God to His people. They made a habit of disobeying God. Habakkuk didn't understand why. He knew it would be better for the people if they followed God.

God wanted people to love each other like He loved them. Instead, they were mean to each other and worshiped idols. This made God sad, but He still loved them.

Habakkuk didn't like seeing people do bad things. He wanted them to change.

"Lord, everything is terrible," Habakkuk said. "Why do You put up with the bad things that the people do? Can You hear me?"

God heard Habakkuk loud and clear. He knew the prophet was upset, so God sent him a message.

"I am going to do something that you won't believe," God said. "I've got a plan. Wait for it."

God told Habakkuk He was going to send mighty warriors to put an end to the people's disobedience.

Habakkuk was worried. He didn't want anyone to get hurt; he just wanted them to obey God.

Habakkuk asked God again: "God, You are so perfect and loving. Why do You let people do bad things? Can You hear me?"

Again, God listened carefully to what Habakkuk asked. He said again, "Wait for it."

Then God gave Habakkuk a vision. It was another message for the people. One day, everyone would be free from evil! Just not yet. God told Habakkuk to trust Him and wait for His timing, even though it was hard.

GOD
IS
GREATEST!

Have you ever had to
wait for something?
It's not easy being
patient. God told
Habakkuk that He was
going to make things
better, but not for a
long time. God always
keeps His promises.
But sometimes we
have to wait.

After God spoke, Habakkuk was filled with hope. He knew God's people would face hard times because of their bad decisions. But he also knew God would lift His people up again.

"OK, God, I will be patient," Habakkuk prayed. "Sometimes I don't know why scary things happen, but I know You always do the right thing. You fill me with joy. You make me strong!"

GOD'S PROMISE to YOU!

When we disobey God, it's called sin. Sin separates us from God. God promised to make a way to save people from sin. He'd send a Savior, the Messiah, who would make our relationship with God right again.

God kept His promise by sending His Son, Jesus, to die on the cross for the sins of the world. Jesus conquered death and rose from grave, so we can have new life and live forever with God in heaven.

If you want to know God personally and be forgiven for your sins, you can say this prayer: "Dear Jesus, I believe You loved me so much that You died on the cross for me. I believe You rose from the dead and can forgive my sins. Please come into my heart and make me Your child. I want to follow and obey You. Amen."

MORE SPIRITUAL DISCIPLESHIP

Strong faith is important to you. So help your family live out God's Word with Focus on the Family's faith-building resources!

Focus on the Family Clubhouse Jr.® magazine is full of fun that will reinforce your family's biblical values. Each issue comes with stories, jokes, activities, and more for kids ages 3-7.

Focus on the Family has dozens of resources for children of all ages! No matter what phase of parenting you're in, we have tools for your family's unique journey.

Find everything here:

Scan to explore